WAYANG: STORIES OF THE SHADOW PUPPETS

KINGS AND GIANTS

Martini Fisher

With a heartfelt thanks to my father,

who has been, and always will be, my mentor

and my best friend.

CONTENT:

INTRODUCTION

The story of the ruler of the three realms continued. Sang Hyang Manikmaya has undergone many reincarnations. Through all his reincarnations, his quick and fiery temper remained, and continued to cause suffering to others. However, he was and would continue to be the ruler of the three realms.

Togog and Semar descended upon earth to find their charges. Togog to find the giants, and Semar to find the kings. The giants, considered big, menacing creatures, more disposed to rage than kindness, they have more in common with mankind than we realized. They experienced passion, love and heartbreak just like anyone we know.

This book also tells the story of the first kings, descended from the gods themselves, trying to build their own places on earth, claiming a little bit of the world ruled by their forefathers. And throughout their lives, the gods weaved their divine presences as if they were silk robes, always soft, but not always bringing happiness.

Martini Fisher, 2014

The Great Battle of the Rice Field

After walking aimlessly for, what seemed to him, forever in and out of the woods and up and down the mountains, Togog met with rows upon rows of heavily armed giants. It was, in fact, ten thousand giants forming an army undertaking a journey to a battlefield.

As he moved to avoid them, a rough and fierce voice called to him, coming from one of the giants who stood at the very front. From his clothing, Togog realized that he was facing none other than King Bubaksalangka, the very king he was looking for.

Lost in his own thought, Togog only stared at the king of the giants until the king's voice woke him from his brief reverie.

"Hey! Answer me, you!" The king boomed roughly.

"Forgive me, king, lordship, big person... man... giant." Togog stammered. *Oh how humiliating*, he thought. *You're the former Sang Hyang Antaga, for goodness sake. Pull yourself together, man.*

"I said, which way to Medang Kemulan?" The king repeated his question. Togog knew that Batara Srigati, son of Batara Wisnu had established a kingdom called Medang Kemulan and ruled the kingdom as Sri Mahapunggung, but he had also heard that King Bubaksangkala wanted to bring war on to the new kingdom. And there he stood bragging to his generals that he would rob and plunder all assets of Medang Kemulan.

"If you'd forgive me, sire, I do not think it is wise to attack Medang Kemulan." Togog advised the king of the giants, "the country is lead by a king who is a direct descendant of the gods, and –" A roar from King Bubaksangkala told him that he was not concerned with Togog's advice. He forced Togog to come along as his guide. Togog had no other choice, so he followed the king's command and led them to Medang Kemulan.

As the convoy moved to the direction of Medang Kemulan through a jungle, it then stalled. In the middle of a narrow path which they were travelling to, stretched a massive sleeping figure blocking the way. It was remarkable. The figure was very large, exceeding even the size of king Bubaksangkala himself.

King Bubaksangkala growled in anger. He immediately gave orders to his troops to forcibly drag the giant figure out of his way. Togog recognized the sleeping figure and stopped the king's order. It was important for them to let the sleeping figure be, because that sleeping figure was none other than Batara Kala, the son of the King of the Three Realms himself. However, for the second time, the king of the giant ignored Togog's advice. He sounded the sign of attack, and the giant army soon besieged the target. Togog shrugged, then hid himself in the bushes to watch the event unfolding before him. He did not want his identity to be known by Batara Kala.

Batara Kala was awakened from his slumber, angry from being disturbed. A battle was inevitable, though clearly unbalanced. The army of Bubaksanglaka attacked Batara Kala from all directions, pouncing like hungry lions ready to rip apart the flesh of their prey. However, although he was surrounded from all sides, Batara Kala was able to defend himself and, in his turn, attack King Bubaksanglaka and his entire army, and ultimately won the battle.

Seeing this, King Bubaksanglaka knelt before Batara Kala, wailing piteously, begging him for mercy and promised to serve him. Batara Kala forgave him and his army. However, King Bubaksanglaka was not being sincere. He influenced Batara Kala to join him in attacking Medang Kemulan, promising him the rule of the kingdom. Batara Kala approved of this and the new alliance then stormed Medang Kemulan. Togog, now forgotten, followed them from afar.

On their way to Medang Kemulan, they were surprised by the appearance of a figure of a woman hovering in the air, sparkling like sunlight. King Bubaksanglaka asked Batara Kala to immediately pursue that woman. He whispered that the woman who was floating in the air will be a very suitable consort of the great Batara Kala when he becomes the king of Medang Kemulan. Hearing this, Batara Kala became curious and pursued the lady.

The goddess was none other than Dewi Srinadi, daughter of Batara Wisnu, who came out of her palace to see her brother, Sri Mahapunggung in Medang Kemulan. But she was lost. In this confusion, Dewi Srinadi was surprised and frightened to see a giant figure pursuing her. A chase ensued in the sky.

Meanwhile, king Bubaksangkala forgot all about Batara Kala who was chasing Dewi Srinadi. Instead, he felt free from Batara Kala, and soon led back his troops to attack Medang Kemulan. However, by coincidence, both Dewi Srinadi and Batara Kala were already in the region of Medang Kemulan. Dewi Srinadi immediately tried to hide herself. By hiding in the mainland, she would be hidden and therefore not so easily visible. Quick as a flash, Dewi Srinadi then dove and disappeared among the rice plants.

Although Batara Kala pretended to look around for his prey, he was quite confident that Dewi Srinadi had been hiding among the rice plant, so he dove into the earth, also hiding his great figure among the rice plants by way of transforming into a large, brown grasshopper perching on a rice plant, intending to look for Dewi Srinadi inconspicuously.

Meanwhile, King Bubaksangkala and troops arrived at Medang Kemulan. King

Bukasangkala planned to create unrest by transforming himself and his troops into rice pests and other animals to destroy the fields. Therefore, they changed their forms and separated, each ruining the rice crops of Medang Kemulan so that the farmers of Medang Kemulan face crop failures, and eventually, all the people of Medang Kemulan would be hungry, weak and easily defeated.

Batara Kala who at this time was stalking his prey, was amazed when suddenly he saw hundreds of pests flew in and ruin millions of rice plants in front of him. The people of Medang Kemulan also felt uneasy. Fearing crop failure, they appealed to Sri Mahapunggung.

Before Sri Mahapunggung, the farmers recounted the events that have taken place. Semar, by this time a trusted servant of the king, recommended that the king meditated and asked his father for directions, because this incident did not seem like a normal and reasonable event.

Sri Mahapunggung followed his advice and meditated. A few moments later, Batara Wisnu appeared before him. To his son, Wisnu said that Medang Kemulan was attacked by a giant force led by King Bubaksanglaka. Sri Mahapunggung immediately ordered his generals, Mahapatih Sadana and Senopati Puring Gading to prepare the troops which he would lead directly.

Before leaving Medang Kemulan, Batara Wisnu first came to the area which was taken over by the pests. He went to one of the rice plant and brought strong winds to blow around the plants. Instantly, from one rice crop emerged Batara Kala. Batara Kala, who had met Batara Wisnu in his disguise as Dalang Kandhabuana, the puppetmaster who broke his weapon so he could no longer kill and eat any living beings. Batara Kala was surprised to see him again. He froze on his place, experiencing an unfamiliar conflict of the heart. On one side, he wanted to fight Batara Wisnu, just like he has fought everyone else. Yet, on another, Dalang Kandhabuana, trickster that he was, was the first person who had been kind to him.

So there he stood indecisively, opening and closing his mouth, wanting to say something. Before Batara Kala could ask any questions, Batara Wisnu, still kind as always, ordered him to face their father, Sang Hyang Jagatnata. Batara Kala obeyed and immediately flew towards heaven Suralaya, where Sang Hyang Jagatnata then reminded him of his responsibility as a husband to Batari Durga.

Meanwhile, the troops of Medang Kemulan were heavily armed, not only with weapons, but with a full range of pest repelling equipment. Let by Sri Mahapunggung, all soldiers tried their best to draw out the pests to turn them back to giants so they could fight them properly. Magnificent amount of pests flew in the air, overwhelming the eyes. Sri Mahapunggung chanted his spell and the pests and vermin transformed back into the giant army forces led by king Bubaksangkala.

Frenzied sounds of gunfires, screams and cries of pain were heard all around. The two mighty generals, Mahapatih Sadana and Senopati Puri Gading were there fighting the enemies. The three sons of Semar: Bagong, Petruk and Gareng, were also there, shoulder to shoulder destroying one giant after the other.

"So, tell me, brothers, when is the celebration starting?" Petruk said as he kicked a giant's large behind.

"Father said this is the celebration, now be quiet and let me hit someone!" Bagong said as he lifted a very heavy mace over his head, looking for a nearby giant

"Hmph. He has bad taste in celebrations." Petruk rolled his eyes as he outran the giant he just kicked.

Meanwhile, King Bubaksangkala came face to face with King Sri Mahapunggung. Both fought very fiercely until Sri Mahapunggung successfully stripped King Bubaksangkala of his magic. All of Medang Kemulan cheered the victory.

Togog tapped Semar on his shoulder. The two brothers embraced each other after being separated for their journeys.

"Patience, brother," Semar gently said to Togog, seeing his brother's drawn and tired face. He remembered how alone Togog was in his journey and was again grateful for his three adopted sons. "Every journey will end one day." Togog could only take a deep breath and smiled.

The Great Scripture

There once was a kingdom called Lokapala. The king of Lokapala was a dashing young man and a highly competent soldier. His name was King Danaraja. The people and the army of Lokapala consisted of both the human and giant race, living in harmony. It was one of the oldest kingdoms in the world and King Danaraja could trace his own lineage all the way back to Sang Hyang Jagatnata himself. His grandfather, King Andanapati, the founder of the kingdom of Lokapala, was the son of Batara Sambodana, and consequently the great grandson of Sang Hyang Jagatnata.

King Danaraja heard of a contest for the hand of a beautiful princess by the name of Dewi Sukesi. Dewi Sukesi is the daughter of the giant King Sumali of the kingdom of Alengka. The beauty of Dewi Sukesi was famous abroad, and it was certain that all of the eligible kings who had heard of Alengka would want to compete.

King Danaraja was no exception. He wanted to win Dewi Sukesi and make her his royal consort of the kingdom of Lokapala.

However, he felt discouraged because the contest that was held by King Sumali was not that of the usual competition of physical combat, but Dewi Sukesi herself has requested that the contest is to search for the person who could unmask the meaning of the great scripture, named *Sastra Jendra Hayu Ningrat Pangruwating Diyu.*

There have been many kings who withdrew from the contest because they were not able to open the curtain. However, King Danaraja felt confident that his father, Resi[1] Wisrawa would be able to unmask the meaning of the great scripture. Therefore, he asked his father to join the competition to represent him.

Resi Wisrawa was a very loving father to his son, and he was only too pleased to grant his son's request. He also agreed that it was, in fact, improper for a king to go directly into the competition arena, especially the competition of the Great Scripture. He said that only he himself who could sufficiently describe the valuable knowledge contained behind that curtain. With sincere love of a father, Resi Wisrawa then went to the kingdom of Alengka to win the hand of Dewi Sukesi for his son.

---

[1] Monk/Wiseman

The kingdom of Alengka was a great empire. King Sumali may be a giant, but his virtue and nobility in spirit and action surpassed even those of human beings. Like King Danaraja, he was also continuing in the footsteps of his ancestors. King Sumali, as was his ancestors, led a country of giants who lived peacefully alongside the humans in the world.

King Sumali had two children. One was a son, a very powerful giant named Prahasta, and the other one was his very beautiful daughter, Dewi Sukesi. This daughter was now the reason of his confusion. He was looking for a mate for his beloved daughter, but she has set a very difficult task for his suitors. The person of whom she would give herself in marriage needed to interpret the great scripture. Not only that, his own brother, Jambumangli, the most powerful giant in the kingdom also set his own additional requirement, that the person also needed to be a warrior who was able to overcome his own power. This made the situation even more difficult, since none of the knights and kings who came to Alengka were able to defeat Jambumangli.

However, Jambumangli had his own reason to set that requirement. He wanted Dewi Sukesi for himself. He did not one any one else to have her. Clever Dewi Sukesi knew this, which was why she set the one requirement which could not be met by Jambumangli.

Resi Wisrawa finally reached the kingdom of Alengka and met with King Sumali. Resi Wisrawa knew King Sumali very well. They were in fact close friends. The king told him, that to obtain the hand of Dewi Sukesi, it did not matter who the person was, or where he came from, he needed to be able to interpret the *Sastra Jendra Hayuningrat Pangruwating Diyu.* Resi Wisrawa agreed.

"Indeed, my friend. It will give me great pleasure to teach the meaning of Sastra Jendra to Dewi Sukesi." Resi Wisrawa said.

"What, you don't mean to say that you understand the content?" King Sumali asked him, puzzled.

Resi Wisrawa then gave his friend a little glimpse of the meaning of the Sastra Jendra.

"*Sastra Jendra Hayuningrat Pangruwating Diyu* is, in fact, the secret of the universe. He who was able to read, understand and implement the teachings of the scripture will achieve perfection in his life. He who was aware of the true meaning of the teachings contained in it will be able to recognize the passions of the self. This would enable him to further nurture his own desires, under the leadership of his own good conscience, and obliterated any trace of evil within him under the direction of sublime wisdom."

King Sumali was stunned at Resi Wisrawa's description. Although the explanation he heard was brief, but it greatly affected his heart. King Sumali immediately invited Resi Wisrawa to Dewi Sukesi's chamber. There, after dismissing all her attendants, Resi Wisrawa explained to Dewi Sukesi the meaning of every word contained in *Sastra Jendra Hayuningrat Pangruwating Diyu*. There was no one else in the room apart from Resi Wisrawa and Dewi Sukesi, so that the knowledge could be absorbed perfectly by Dewi Sukesi.

Sastra Jendra Hayuningrat Pangruwating Diyu was more than the key to understanding the contents of the universe. It also contained the meaning of men's relationship with the almighty Creator, men's relationships with their fellow men, as well as the universe in which they lived. It was the one thing which contained the truth, nobility, perfection and majesty that had not been within the reach of ordinary people. Therefore, the great scripture helps one to achieve the perfection in life, and directs one on his return to his Creator after death. `

Meanwhile, in heaven Suralaya, Sang Hyang Jagatnata observed this new development with concern. Dewi Sukesi's demand of knowing the essence of the scripture disturbed him greatly. His concern quickly turned to anger at Resi Wisrawa's attempt to explain the great scripture. He did not want any human being, or any creature in the universe to know the meaning of the great scripture, because if they succeed in gaining that knowledge, there will be neither men, djinns nor giants who would ever make any sacrifices to the gods.

Therefore, Sang Hyang Jagatnata planned to thwart Resi Wisrawa's lesson. Together with his new daughter in law, Batari Durga who recently married Batara Kala, Sang Hyang Jagatnata descend upon earth towards Alengka. In the darkness of night, in a chamber only illuminated by small candles, two figures sat for their study. Resi Wisrawa started his interpretation of the great scripture before Dewi

Sukesi who listened to him with complete focus.

Unnoticed by the two humans, two little lights emerged from the two lit candles and made their way towards them The two heavenly lights continued to break into the bodies of Resi Wisrawa and Dewi Sukesi to take over their souls. Those two lights were none other than Sang Hyang Jagatnata who entered the body of Resi Wisrawa, and Batari Durga, who entered the body of Dewi Sukesi.

Deep within the two bodies now laid two beings who sought to exploit the lust within the two humans' nature. Batari Durga affected the passions of Dewi Sukesi, and Sang Hyang Jagatnata affected the same desires in Resi Wisrawa. The temptation burned between the two beings and, before Resi Wisrawa were able to outline the overall essence of the scripture, they have both fallen into the contemptible abyss of unbridled lust.

Both Resi Wisrawa and Dewi Sukesi were defenseless against the influences of Batari Durga and Sang Hyang Jagatnata. Resi Wisrawa had forgotten that he was there only to serve as his son's representative to meet the desired requirements of Dewi Sukesi and thus the *Sastra Jendra Hayuningrat Pangruwating Diyu* could not be completed. Instead of understanding and enlightenment, the result of the meeting was that of shame and disgrace, which would spawn a catastrophic result in the future. However, whatever the result may be, lives still need to be lived.

Therefore, the next day, Resi Wisrawa and Dewi Sukesi faced her father, King Sumali, and told him everything that has occurred. After his initial rage, wise King Sumali accepted the fact that what was done could not be undone. Resi Wisrawa and Dewi Sukesi were then married, and the contest was cancelled.

King Danaraja, enraged by the betrayal of his own father, waged war against the kingdom of Alengka. This war would last for almost a hundred years.

The Ten-faced Giant King

As time passed, the children of Resi Wisrawa and Dewi Sukesi grew into adulthood. The eldest son was named Rahwana, a big tall giant whose face can turn into ten faces when he was angry, the second was Kumbakarna, an even bigger giant whose body exceeded even that of Rahwana's. The third born was Sarpakaneka, a giantess, and the youngest was Gunawan Wibisana, a handsome knight. All four grew, educated by their uncle, Prahasta.

Prahasta was a wise giant who was very fond of his nephews and niece. He gave his affection unreservedly and equally to all four of them. One day, King Sumali told his grandchildren to go to the Gohkarna Mountain to meditate. He wished for them to become knights who would bring pride to his nation. Therefore, the four children of Resi Wisrawa went to the Gohkarna Mountain and chose their individual places to meditate.

Four of them had their own special way of meditating. Rahwana meditated by standing with his left foot lifted, one hand reaching up to the sky and his other hand crossing over his chest. Kumbakarna meditated by sleeping. His body, which resembles a large amount of hills, lied between the mountain valleys of Gohkarna. Sarpakaneka positioned her body in such a way that she was standing on her head and had her feet on top, while Gunawan Wibisana's form of meditation was that of a lotus position. For decades, the sons and daughter of Resi Wisrawa diligently performed their penances.

In the fifth year, mount Candradimuka was shaken with a great force. Incandescent rocks and lava spatter heat of fire, and black smoke diffused the peak of Tengguru. Heaven Suralaya were clouded over by jet black clouds. The gods and goddesses inhabitants of the heaven were screaming in panic in the unfriendly occurrences of mount Candradimuka.

Sang Hyang Jagatnata asked Batara Narada about what was frightening the inhabitants of heaven. By using their powers they saw the source of the disturbance. Mount Candradimuka has been shaken by the meditations of the four children of Resi Wisrawa in the mountain of Gohkarna. Sang Hyang Jagatnata then invited Batara Narada to meet them and asked them directly what their intentions were.

At the top of the mountain Gohkarna, never before visited by humans, Sang Hyang Jagatnata and Batara Narada met with Rahwana, the eldest son of Resi Wisrawa. His eyes have been closed for fifty years.

Now those eyes were wide open, watching two divine beings that radiated power and serenity. After knowing that the two forms standing before him were none other than Sang Hyang Jagatnata, the ruler of the three realms, and Batara Narada, the great general of the three realms, asking him why he would spend decades meditating, Rahwana made his request.

Rahwana wished to have supernatural powers and richness exceeding anyone on earth. He wished that he would not be defeated by beings such as djinns or demons, humans and even the gods in heaven. He also wished to be as great as the Gohkarna Mountain, and for his old age to be stretched over that of a thousand elephants, a thousand dragons, and over seven times the life of mortals. This request was approved by Sang Hyang Jagatnata, despite the misgivings of Batara

Narada who warned him of a disaster if Rahwana's desires were fulfilled.

Sang Hyang Jagatnata and Batara Guru continued their journey and met Kumbakarna, the second son of Resi Wisrawa, who was sleeping on the valley of Gohkarna. Sang Hyang Jagatnata woke him from his sleep and asked him of his desire. Unlike his brother, Kumbakarna did not want anything. He wanted no magic to defeat his enemies. He wanted to sleep, eat and do all the simple pleasures he enjoyed so much. He wished to live simply and comfortably, without having to disturb the tranquility of other people's lives. Sang Hyang Jagatnata granted his request and gave him a prolonged drowsiness.

Sensing four major presences in the mountain, Sang Hyang Jagatnata and Batara Narada continued their journey to find the third force in meditation. They found and wake Sarpakaneka, the giantess, third born of Resi Wisrawa. She happily requested supernatural powers and strength equal of that of the gods as well as the fulfillment of all her desires. These wishes were also granted by Sang Hyang Jagatnata.

The two deities then met Gunawan Wibisana. To their surprise, the fourth son of Resi Wisrawa did not ask for any miracle. All he wanted was wisdom and understanding of the dharma. This wish was also granted.

After reaping the results of asceticism, the four offsprings of Resi Wisrawa came back home to their beloved country of Alengka. The first born, Rahwana was then crowned as the new king of Alengka.

The Two Kingdoms

Upon the death of Resi Wisrawa in the hand of his own son, King Danaraja, the war between Lokapala and Alengka was now over. The kingdom of Alengka handed all its political rights, as well as the fate of its people under the care of of Lokapala. Despite this situation, King Danaraja gave King Rahwana the rights of Alengka's policies. King Danaraja acknowledged the existence of the son who had been born of Dewi Sukesi and his father. They were brothers of the blood which means King Rahwana was his younger siblings. King Danaraja also thought there was no reason to punish them, because they never knew of the sin done by their parents.

Therefore, for a time, King Danaraja appointed Prahasta as a regent, who would govern until such time that the sons and daughter of Dewi Sukesi and Resi Wirawa matured so the governments of Alengka could be handed to them. Although a giant, Prahasta was guided by a good conscience. He did not have an envious nature and thirst for power. Prahasta was wise, just like his father, King

Sumali who now lived as a hermit, who had now retreated from worldliness.

Then came the military expansion of Lokapala to other countries such as Sinhala, Pandya, Malawa, Kerala, and many others. Many countries were brought to their knees by Lokapala, making the rule of King Danaraja famous as the golden age of Lokapala. Unfortunately, King Danaraja was a little too fond of luxury and materialism. This vice would prove to be his downfall.

One of King Danaraja's greatest wish was to obtain Dewi Danuwati, the consort of King Kertawirya of the kingdom of Maespati. The great Maespati was not included in Lokapala's colony. Therefore, there was no reason for King Danaraja to attack King Kertawirya if he did not conform to his wishes.

King Danaraja sent Gohmuka as his ambassador to Maespasti. Gohmuka is a giant retainer of Lokapala, most trusted by King Danaraja in performing any duties, attacking and conquering countries which have now become subordinates and allies of Lokapala. Armed with a few hundred soldiers, Gohmuka left for the kingdom of Maespati.

Unaware of these developments, King Kertawirya was a very happy man, because his days were the days of waiting. He was eagerly waiting for the birth of his son, the crown prince who would be born from the womb of a Dewi Danuwati. A crown prince who would replace his position in the future to continue the ideals of his ancestors.

But King Kertawirya's excitement faded at the arrival of an ambassador of Lokapala in his palace. Without any preambles, Gohmuka conveyed his message to King Kertawirya. The King of Lokapala demanded of him to bring Dewi Danuwati to Lokapala to be presented to the king, because King Danaraja wanted Dewi Danuwati to be his consort.

King Kertawirya was very surprised to hear the intent and purpose of Gohmuka. Moreover, Gohmuka made a threat against him, that there would be a sea of fire in Maespati if King Kertawirya refused the desire of the King of Lokapala. King Kertawirya, in anger, chose to take up arms rather than surrender his honor and dignity.

Before the king could act, the general of Maespati, Mahapatih Gumiyat immediately dragged Gohmuka to the palace square. Fighting ensued between Gohmuka and Mahapatih Gumiyat. Gohmuka held resistance with just a few hundred soldiers, lunging himself forward to face the strength of Mahapatih Gumiyat and the army of Maespati.

Although Gohmuka was skilled enough in the battlefield, he could not compete with Mahapatih Gumiyat. Many times Gohmuka fell, struck by the blows of his magic. There was no significant resistance from the retainer of Lokapala. Finally, along with a few remaining soldiers he decided to run away leaving Maespati, returning home to his country to report the incident to King Danaraja.

After hearing the report of Gohmuka, King Danaraja immediately ordered his general, Mahapatih Wisnungkara to prepare the entire army Lokapala. King Danaraja commanded that Maespati should be a sea of fire. Some countries, allies of Lokapala, participated in the attack. They were all united under the banner of Lokapala to destroy Maespati. Tens of thousands of armed soldiers marched towards Maespati.

Meanwhile, in Maespati, King Kertawirya was aware of the impending danger. He prepared himself for the arrival of the enemy. Together, Mahapatih Gumiyat and King Kertawirya prepared all Maespati's forces. He recognized the power of Lokapala's sizeable army, as well as its support of foreign countries who have become its allies. He knew it would be very difficult for Maespati to be able to win the battle. However, King Kertawirya been determined to maintain his honor and dignity as a king. It was better to be dead than alive as a colonized land. Therefore, to deal with a large force of Lokapala, King Kertawirya asked the help of a powerful sage named Resi Swandageni from the Ardisekar. Resi Swandageni was still related to King Kertawirya by way of his grandfather.

The forces of Lokapala had attacked engaged in the boundary. Their arrival was immediately greeted by the army of Maespati led by King Kertawirya himself, accompanied by Resi Swandageni and Mahapatih Gumiyat. Two forces have brought together weapons of destructions. They attacked each other, lunged, hit, stabbing each other, equally slaying their opponents.

The forces of Lokapala had indeed been tested in every battle, forged with various experiences of war. Moreover, the strength of Lokapala has doubled because it was supported by allies who were always ready to help. On the other hand, the magic of Resi Swandageni had given more strength to the soldiers of Maespati. Resi Wisanggeni was able to recreate the force Maespati's soldiers and multiply it so both forces become balanced.

Mahapatih Wisnuwungkur was a cunning giant magic guru who had a wide range of black magic. Fighting for Lokapala, he created animals which were deadly poisonous. Many soldiers of Maespati fell by the hands of the magic of Mahapatih Wisnuwungkur.

While King Kertawirya was dealing directly with King Danaraja, Mahapatih Gumiyat faced the brunt of Gohmuka and the kings allied to Lokapala. King Danaraja had proven his power as the ruler of Lokapala. With his power, he could not die with a variety of weapons used by King Kertawirya. With each hit, he seemed to be only getting stronger. It was like King Danaraja had a thousand lives. He simply could not die.

Mahapatih Gumiyat who, by this time, in his own battle have managed to kill Gohmuka, saw King Kertawirya's trouble in facing King Danaraja. He therefore immediately pursued and assisted his king Kertawirya.

At the same time, when the King Danaraja attacked Mahapatih Gumiyat, a soldier of Maespati gave a message to King Kertawirya that the queen had given birth to a son. King Kertawirya was very excited. Even if he would have to bear the defeat in the war against Lokapala, but he would not regret it after seeing his long awaited son. Once that occurred to King Kertawirya, he immediately left the battlefield to see his son, while King Danaraja was battling Mahapatih Gumiyat.

In the palace of Maespati, King Kertawirya went straight to his queen's chamber. In her arms was his handsome new son. With all the pride and affection of a new father, King Kertawirya held his son. He then gave him the name Arjunasasrabahu. After the name left his mouth, appeared Batara Narada before him. Batara Narada told King Kertawirya that his son was the incarnation of Batara Wisnu who will destroy all the injustice of his realm. Batara Narada then gave him an heirloom, a legacy of Batara Wisnu which would accompany his son to suppress all forms of crime. King Kertawirya was very excited to hear the narrative of Batara Narada. He soon returned to the battlefield carrying the heritage.

King Danaraja was surprised to see Batara Wisnu's heirloom in the hand of King Kertawirya. The same heritage which was not only feared by the kings, knights or brahmins, but also respected by the gods. King Danaraja briefly doubted his own power against the heirloom, but he was determined to deal with the heritage of magic that even with his own eyes he had watched destroyed a massive part of his troops.

After defeating Mahapatih Gumiyat, just before King Danaraja moved to kill him, suddenly came Batara Narada blocking King Danaraja intervening in the battle. Batara Narada reminded him that there had been a lot of casualties on both sides, especially from Lokapala. Allied kings and people who put their trusts upon Lokapala have now been destroyed. This was the result of the battle caused by greedy appetite that could not be controlled.

Batara Narada advised King Danaraja,

told him to re-live a straight life. There is no benefit in fondness of showing off the power and strength because it will only bring afflictions to many. Batara Narada advised King Danaraja to undergo purification, atone for his sins and mistakes that have been done so far, because after all he was a descendant of the great sage that had become a model on earth.

King Danaraja obeyed Batara Narada's advice, he immediately withdrew his troops from the territory of Maespati back home to his country, and underwent his penance on the banks of the river Ganges.

The Betrayal of a Brother

There was a sense of worry in Prahasta after Rahwana was crowned the king of Alengka. The concern was not caused by jealousy of his inheritance of the throne, but the behavior of King Rahwana which were increasingly worse, and did not reflect the attitude of a king. King Rahwana was very stubborn, unruly and selfish. Sometimes he did not hesitate to hand down harsh punishments to his own retainers in Alengka and renegade their possessions. And when he knew that his parents have been killed by the attacks of king Danaraja, then King Rahwana decided to attack Lokapala.

Prahasta, in his capacity as governor of Alengka as well as foster parent to the king could only give advice. The same with Kumbakarna and Gunawan Wibisana, who opposed the desire of Rahwana who wanted to attack Lokapala, because after all, the king Lokapala was their eldest brother by way of their father, Resi Wisrawa.

King Rahwana not only ignored the advice of his uncle and brothers, he denied them completely. King Rahwana led tens of thousands of troops to attack Lokapala. War raged. King Danaraja moved from his meditation on the banks of river Gange after hearing his country was attacked by the King Rahwana of Alengka. A massive war ensued between Alengka and Lokapala. King Danaraja reminded King Rahwana to withdraw his forces, as he did not want bloodshed among families.

King Rahwana ignored the words of King Danaraja and continued to attack, even hunt, King Danaraja himself. A duel ensued between the two brothers. The two sons of Resi Wisrawa attacked each other, pitting their magic against each other. King Rahwana did not hesitate to injure King Danaraja, repeatedly slammed his magic to his body until the body of the great king of Lokapala was dismembered.

However, the body of King Danaraja which had been mutilated miraculously reunited as a whole without a trace of injury. His recovery from his death made him wonder. Again and again, King Rahwana beheaded King Danaraja. Yet, the gallant king was back from the dead all the time. King Rahwana spared no effort in destroying King Danaraja, but it was all in vain.

King Danaraja's recovery from his death worried the giant king. Again and again King Rahwana beheaded King Danaraja. Yet, the gallant king came back from the dead each time. Every effort has been made to destroy King Danaraja. Until King Rahwana lost his magic, and fell down by a powerful blow from King Danaraja. His whole body turned limp and he fell to the ground.

Moaning in a state of helplessness, King Rahwana could only beg for forgiveness. As King Danaraja came towards him to finish him off, Prahasta suddenly came and knelt before King Danaraja, begging him to forgive King Rahwana of all his faults.

Given the blood relationship between them, King Danaraja finally forgive King Rahwana. Prahasta advised King Rahwana to swallow his pride and go along with King Danaraja to Lokapala, to receive teachings from his eldest brother and become a better knight and king. King Danaraja, pleased with this idea, welcomed his brother with open arms.

After years of living with King Danaraja, King Rahwana gained a wide range of sciences from King of Danaraja. Almost all of King Danaraja's magic was absorbed by King Rahwana. King Danaraja, who at this time was already tired of living as a king, wanted to return to his meditation, then gave his last magic which had been residing in his body to King Rahwana.

King Rahwana was very happy to obtain all of his brother's powers. These powers were famous throughout the universe. Unfortunately, King Rahwana was still the same, vicious king he was many years ago. Realising his new found powers, his desire for revenge was rekindled. He remembered his intent and purpose to wreak revenge against King Danaraja and proved his own power. To his brother's surprise, King Rahwana struck a blow at King Danaraja.

The brothers were then involved in a duel for the second time. But now King Rahwana had the definite advantage. He had inherited all the magic of King Danaraja, and due to his training and living in Lokapala, he was also very familiar with his brother's strengths and weaknesses. King Danaraja was dealt with a final blow from King Rahwana, and not having his powers, truly died. After his death, according to some versions, King Danaraja became a deity. He was renamed Batara Kowera.

The Tragedy of Anjali, Subali and Sugriwa

In the Agrastina hermitage, in the area of Mount Sukendra, there lived a sage named Gotama and his family. It was said that Resi Gotama was a descendant of Sang Hyang Ismaya. He was the son of King Heriya of Maespati, the brother of King Kartawirya, and the uncle of King Arjunasasrabahu. For his services and devotion to the gods, Resi Gotama was awarded a celestial nymph named Dewi Indradi. Struck by her beauty, he took this nymph for his wife. From their marriage, they were blessed with three children. They were the beautiful Dewi Anjani, and the handsome twins, Guwasa and Guwarsi

Years passed, Dewi Indradi, who often felt lonely being married to an old Brahmin who spent most of his time meditating, succumbed to the temptation of the sun god, Batara Surya. And so began years of a clandestine love affair that was so neatly covered, that it was never suspected by her husband, Resi Gotama and her three children.

Dewi Indradi had a divine heirloom, Cupumanik[2] Astagina, given to her by her lover, Batara Surya. When giving her the Cupumanik, Batara Surya cautioned her to never show it to others, not even to her own children. If this message was ignored, there will be disaster. The Cupumanik Astagina is an heirloom of the gods, which under the terms of the gods should not be seen or owned by a common man. This prohibition was because, in addition to having incredible magic properties, it also contained the secret of the real nature of life and nature of beings. When one opened the Cupumanik Astagina, the inside of the bowl will show a stunning picture of the earth, full of colorful enchantments. While on the inside lid there was a variety of stunning panoramas in the entire universe, complementing each other like the scenic view in real life. Whoever saw it would feel as if they were being magically carried by a divine force, enjoying the natural beauty of the altitude, the mountain looked bluish, verdant forests, winding rivers, and soothing blue sky.

However, one day when Dewi Indradi was busy observing the beauty of the content of the Cupumanik, her eldest daughter Dewi

---

[2] Container

Anjani caught her, and of course would like to know what object had caught her mother's interest. She forced Dewi Indradi to lend it to her. Dewi Indradi relented, on the condition that it was not to be known by her brothers. However, Dewi Anjani finally could not resist showing it off to her siblings, Guwarsa and Guwarsi. Consequently, the Cupumanik Astagina became a boon of contention, causing commotion among the three siblings. Dewi Anjani, crying, reported this to her mother, while Guwarsa and Guwarsi complained to their father. Driven by their emotions, Guwarsa and Guwarsi accused their father of unfairly favoring Dewi Anjani by giving gifts that they did not get themselves.

The allegations of his two sons made Resi Gotama sad and concerned, since he never did anything like that. Soon he called Dewi Anjani and Dewi Indradi. Due to her fear and respect to her father, Dewi Anjani handed the Cupumanik Antagina to her father, telling him frankly that she acquired the object from her mother.

Meanwhile, Dewi Indradi stayed silent, not daring to tell her husband the truth about how she obtained the divine object. She realized, however, that she was caught between a rock and a hard place. Her honesty would expose her affair with Batara Surya, while her silence would show her lack of respect to her husband. It was this very silence of Dewi Indradi which made Resi Gotama angry. At the height of his emotion, he said, "Speak, woman. Do not stand there in silence like a statue!"

The good Resi Gotama did not realize the full extent of his powers, gained from years of meditation. After he said that, his wife did in fact turn into a human-sized rock in the shape of Dewi Indradi.

There was nothing the Resi or his daughter could do to bring back Dewi Indradi. In sadness, Resi Gotama threw the stone monument as far as possible. The stone feel in the park near the kingdom of Alengka. One day, this curse would end when the stone was used to defend the truth.

For the sake of justice for his three children, Resi Gotama then tossed the Cupumanik into the air. As the Cupumanik disappeared, Resi said this, that whoever finds the Cupumanik later would be the rightful owner. Thus, Dewi Anjani, Guwarsi and Guwarsa ran, each pursuing the heritage of the gods. But this Cupumanik seemed as if it had wings. Very soon, it had drifted across the hills. The Cupumanik then separated into two, the bowl itself fell to the ground and transformed into a lake named Nirmala, while the lid fell and formed the lake Sumala.

Meanwhile Dewi Anjani, Guwarsi and Guwarsa thought that the Cupumanik fell into the already existing lake in the middle of the forest. According to legends, parts of the bodies of the person who were overcome with a sense of worldliness and greed when touching the water of the lake will be turned into a part of the body of an ape.

Without thinking, the twins, Guwarsa and Guwarsi immediately plunged into the lake, looking for the container. Dewi Anjani who were not as brave as her brothers stood at the edge of the lake, stunned.

Then, the exhaustion which was due after her exertion caught up with her, and Dewi Anjani then bent over to wash her face with the water of the lake to refresh herself. She dipped her arms into the water, and as she pulled her arms out of the water, she screamed.

She saw bushy furs from her hands all the way up to her elbows. As she panics and splashed the water about, her face and the rest of her body gradually turned to that of a monkey.

She cried and cried. She shed further tears also for her brothers, who at that moment came to the surface of the lake also in the form of apes. What a catastrophe! The three siblings were devastated. The beauty and loveliness of Dewi Anjani was no more. There were also no more of the dazzling faces of Guwarsa and Guwarsi.

There is something about tragedies which reminds mankind of their humanity as well as brotherhood. The three siblings, who were always somewhat distant from each other, now embraced their siblings, crying on each other's shoulders and offering comfort. With their hearts heavy with regret, they went back home and asked their father if he could restore them.

Resi Gotama noticed the change in his children. Gone were their aggressions and demanding presence. They approached him with humility and surrender to their faiths. Yes, Resi Gotama was saddened by their physical changes, however, he could not help but feel a bit of hope for his children's nobility of characters.

"I cannot change you, my children," he said gently, squeezing Dewi Anjani's hand, before she brought his hand to her temple as a sign of respect, "There is no power on this earth that can change you back. However, although you are apes in your physical forms, you are still blessed with your human hearts. Develop your hearts, and you shall find happiness whatever your forms may be." And with that, the three siblings said their goodbyes to their father. They would again leave home, only this time, they would perform penances to purify themselves.

Dewi Anjani was to perform her penance in a river. She would meditate in the middle of the river flow like a frog. Guwarsi and Guwarsa were given new names by their father. Guwarsi became known as Subali, and he was tasked to perform his penance in a Mountain, hanging on branches of tall trees like a bat. Guwarsa became known as Sugriwa. He performed his penance in a forest. He occupied a little field of grass in the middle of the forest like a deer.

Thus, the three siblings underwent their meditations for a very long time to make up for their mistakes.

The Man with the White Blood

This story begins with a young hermit who had successfully helped the gods to quell the unrest in heaven. His name was Bambang Anggana Putra. For his services Anggana was blessed by Sang Hyang Jagatnata, who has undergone his latest incarnation and now known as Batara Guru, by being allowed to marry one of his celestial goddesses.

In the heavenly palace of Jonggring Salaka, the gods assembled, awaiting the words of the King of the Three Realms. Batara Guru said, "My son, Anggana, as promised, upon your services to quell the unrest in heaven Suralaya, I will bestow upon you a goddess to take as your wife. Choose ye one among these goddesses."

Obtain grace and honor of the King of the Three Realms was beyond Anggana's wildest dreams. His heart felt like it was going to explode from joy, flattered by the honor granted to him by the deities, that of the freedom to choose any goddess to be his wife.

He is of a virtuous, honest, and innocent disposition. He was so pure that his blood was white. However, he was still human. And as such, retained at least one of humanity's weaknesses, which is a playful nature which sometimes he left unchecked.

"Please, my lord... I am a really very happy servant blessed by heaven, especially with your offer to choose one goddess to marry, but I saw that the goddesses were all flawless, and I am not able to make the choice, but nevertheless , your humble servant ever admire one of them ".

"Who is it, Anggana? I have given you the opportunity to choose."

"If you do not mind, the choice fell on the goddess Uma, an angel who had caught my eye."

A lightning struck. The body of Batara Guru shook, his face flushed, his heart became hot as hot crater of Mount Candradimuka. All the gods gasped hearing the words of Bambang Anggana.

"The universe's honey was dedicated to you, but instead you give me the cup of poison. How dare you, Anggana." Batara Guru could not control his anger, he was offended by the wish of Anggana who he thought had tarnished his authority as the king of the three realms. Imagine, the goddess Uma is the queen of heaven Suralaya, the empress of Batara Guru himself.

Seeing Batara Guru's anger, Anggana immediately genuflected. "Oh my god ... I'm sorry, my lord. I did not intend to insult the dignity of your excellency, I intended it only as a joke because you asked me to choose one goddess in this heavenly realm without exception, I your humble servant was just teasing your majesty, because the goddess Uma herself is a goddess. Please forgive my rudeness."

It may be easy to extinguish a burning fire, but it is difficult to smother the fire of anger in one's heart. Anger never arises without a reason, even if that reason is not always true. And whatever Anggana said could not reduce the anger in Batara Gurus heart.

"Although your nature is commendable, you do not have manners. You have tarnished my authority with a mere joke. A sage like yourself should not have such properties. It is the property of *Duruwiksa*." *Duruwiksa* means "a giant with a savage temper," and as soon as Batara Guru spat that word, smoke came out of his mouth, surrounding Anggana and turned him into a giant. The assembly of the gods and goddesses gasped in fear seeing his new form.

"Please my lord ... Please, please my lord, consider the penalty you have chosen for your servant's mistake. Please return your servant to his previous form. Please my lord." Anggana was devastated to see the change in him. He cried and cried for forgiveness.

"My decision is absolute. Get thee to exile. I shall keep my promise and bestow upon you a goddess for you to take as a wife. She is Dewi Darmastuti, and she will be a companion of your days in exile. However, as soon as she has given birth to your child, she will return here, to heaven."

Batara Narada was stunned to hear the words of the king of the three realms and very concerned about the state of Anggana. "For pity's sake, my liege. Haven't you punished him enough? After all he has done for us, you snatched his happiness by changing him into a giant. Please consider. Keep your heart and mind away from passion and anger so that your words do not overtake your mind."

But his will is done. Nothing and no one could change the mind of Batara Guru anymore. Anggana was very sad. He did not expect to be punished in such a way. After one last tribute, Anggana left heaven and headed towards his exile.

Even after watching the giant figure of Bambang Anggana Putra walking away to the exile he had imposed upon him, Batara Guru still held a grudge. Quietly, he entered into the bowels of the earth, penetrating the earth layers. There, he took a little piece of skin of the Dragon King Antaboga. The skin of Antaboga renewed itself every 1000 years. With his divine power, Batara Guru turned the skin of Dragon King into a very powerful dragon. The king commanded this dragon to stop Anggana's journey and destroy him. The dragon immediately darted away, in pursuit of Bambang Anggana Putra.

Anggana was still hovering in the air, on his way home, when the dragon with incredible speed overtook him. He quickly darted out of the bottom of the earth and immediately ambushed the body of Anggana. He tore into Anggana's body and slammed downwards from the air. Anggana crashed into the earth, crushing into the mountain rocks.

The dragon was not finished with him. He quickly approached Anggana's body and quickly attacked again by spitting poison and fire out of his mouth. The fiery poison melted the rocks and the soils were enveloped in flame. However, the toxins were not able to kill

Anggana, nor was the fire able to burn it. Anggana was not injured at all.

Anggana rose to defend himself. Several times, the dragon wrapped himself around Anggana, wanting to crush his bones. However, he was unsuccessful. It was as if Anggana's giant body had a strength exceeding a troop of elephants. In the end, the dragon was no match for the magic of Anggana. He caught the great dragon by the neck and tore up his mouth, splitting his head into two. The dragon vanished without a trace and turned into a giant figure.

The giant incarnation of the dragon attacked Anggana. The two magical giants plunged into battle with equal passion. For a moment, it was almost as if the battle between the two was balanced since they were equally agile and nimble, yet Anggana then succeded in stabbing his enemy, thereby killing the giant incarnation of the dragon.

However, Batara Guru had considered Anggana's strength, and had prepared for what just occurred. It was amazing! Every drop of blood that came out of the giant body of the dragon incarnation, which had now soaked the grass, rocks and the surfaces near the two warriors transformed into ten great giants, each and every one of them similar in appearance with the one just killed. Anggana looked on in amazement. His body froze in shock.

Those giants attacked him. Anggana was surrounded and attacked from all directions. He tried to resist, but as soon as he killed one giant, the giant's droplets of blood turned into yet another giant. The more giants he injured, and the more blood was shed, the more giants appeared. Feeling that there was nothing more he could do, Anggana immediately ran away to avoid the giant army siege.

After reaching a safe enough distance, Anggana calmed himself by meditating in silence. He meditated for, and only for, his own calmness of mind, surrendering, accepting his impending death if needs by, reducing all his desires, uniting his heart and mind. He was of pure heart, and unwittingly, by sincerely undergoing his meditation, Bambang Anggana Putra showed his true identity which was as pure as the flowing white blood in his body. Smooth breeze forming a white light radiating his body.

The giants saw the white light from afar and approached. As they came closer, instantly the giants merged back into one. And that giant reincarnation of the dragon dropped down to his knee in awe. "Great Resi," he said,

"I... I can not fight you. It was wrong of me to fight one with white blood."

Anggana, after his meditation, no longer felt fear nor anger. He was serenity itself. Still, closing his eyes, sitting in front of the giant. The giant said, "Let me serve you great one. If you ever need me, invoke me, and I shall come." After he said this, a flash of light surrounded his body, and the giant incarnation of the dragon infiltrated the body of Anggana, uniting his soul to the pure man, thus forever serving the man with the white blood.

A few days later, as promised by the king of the three realms, Dewi Darmastuti was sent down from heaven. The goddess was then married to Bambang Anggana, and they lived together in harmony. Loving and cherishing each other. Although the shape and form of Anggana was now that of a giant, the goddess loved him devotedly. This seed of love and devotion bore fruit and Dewi Darmastuti gave birth to a child.

The child was a girl, who inherited her mother's beauty and brought complete joy to the happy couple. But, their happiness immediately subsided when they remembered of the words of Batara Guru, that the goddess will return home to heaven after she gave birth to a child. Anggana's tears were biter sweet. He was a new father to a beautiful baby girl, yet he lost his beautiful and much loved wife, as Dewi Darmastuti must leave him and their child behind. Their happiness forcibly taken away by the anger of the King of the Three Realms.

And so, Bambang Anggana Putra lived alone with his daughter, who he named Pujawati, a name which means "devotion." He lavished his daughter with love and affection. His gentleness to his daughter and determination to make a better future for her touched the hearts of the gods in heaven, except Batara Guru who still held a grudge him, and believed by all who knew him that he would continue to bear this grudge for the rest of Bambang Anggana's life.

Because of his devotion, Batara Narada renamed Bambang Anggana as Bagaspati, which means "the sun's ray." That was indeed what Bagaspati was to his daughter. He shines upon his daughter, cultivating her spirit, provided her with livelihood, and protect her lovingly to the end of his life.

The Girl from the Mountain

Mandaraka was a wealthy kingdom, with fertile grounds and happy people. It was led by a king named King Mandrapati. His consort was Dewi Tejawati. The royal couple was blessed with two children. The first was a son named Bambang Narasoma, and the second was a daughter named Dewi Madrim.

One day, King Mandrapati invited his son, Bambang Narasoma to talk about his wedding. For a very long time, King Mandrapati had been dreaming about holding his own grandchild in his arms, but Narasoma was still unwilling to find himself a wife. Although the king had often tried to persuade him, even matchmaking him with the daughters of kings and nobles, but Narasoma always declined politely.

"Father, I hope I do not offend you by declining your good intention towards me. I will marry, I am certain of it, only that I still have not found a woman whom my heart desires."

"What sort of woman is she that your heart desires, my son?" The king asked him eagerly.

"I desire a woman who is similar to my mother, the queen." Narasoma said.

This answer startled the king. The king's fault is his quick temper, making him jump to hasty conclusions and thinks the worst in people. Even his own son. He considered, by answering in this manner, that his son had been insubordinate towards himself and his queen. But, Narasoma was referring to similarities of personality with his mother. Her gentleness and affection towards her children and her loyalty to her husband. Before he could tell his father this, King Mandrapati accused him of being absurd, pointing his finger at him in hasty anger. Because of his wrath, King Mandrapati expelled Narasoma from the palace and did not allow his son home before finding a woman to be his wife.

Narasoma was a good boy, devoted to his family. He was very fond to his mother and sister, and very protective of them. Before leaving the palace, Narasoma visited his mother and sister and told them all about his father's misunderstanding. Dewi Tejawati and Dewi Madrim were very concerned, because they understood what Narasoma was looking for and what he really meant when he said that he wanted someone similar to his mother. As he said his goodbyes to them, Narasoma promised to return to Mandaraka after finding the woman who later would become his wife.

Narasoma then wandered. In his wanderings, he saw many things outside the palace which he had never seen before. Narasoma had spent his whole life in the palace, and therefore unfamiliar with the people and the world beyond the palace walls. He felt free as a bird flying at will, without any of those palace rules shackling and confining him. From here on, he could learn for himself and seek new experiences, learn various kinds of knowledge of the natural environment so that later he would become a more mature and worthy king.

As we leave Narasoma to his wandering, Resi Bagaspati and his beloved daughter Pujawati still lived happily together. As time went on, Pujawati had grown into a mature, beautiful girl with a face of an angel. Under her father's guidance, she grew up to be a good girl, loyal and very obedient to her father.

One day, Pujawati was dreaming in her sleep, of meeting a handsome knight who was able to capture her heart. The dream occurred repeatedly, making Pujawati a bit heart sick. A growing expectation rose in this sweet girl of love, and she spent her days in reverie.

Seeing his beloved daughter daydreaming alone day after day, Resi Bagaspati was very concerned. Maybe Pujawati missed her mother? He wondered. It was the child's unfortunate fate that she never knew her mother. She never saw her mother's beautiful face, just hearing stories of her mother from him before falling asleep, clutching her simple doll which Resi Bagaspati made for her from the roots of a big tree, closing her eyes and beautifully drifted off to sleep. Resi Bagaspati would often watched her sleep and pray that perhaps she would be able to see her mother in her dreams. That, in her dreams at least, she would feel even for a brief moment that she had both of her parents together with not a care in the world.

"My daughter Pujawati, what is it that disturbs your heart and mind that I often see you daydreaming? Tell me, daughter. It saddens me to see you like this. Do you miss your mother?" Finally, Resi Bagaspati asked his daughter.

Pujawati shook her head slowly, "I do not miss her, father. I know I will never be able to see her and I am at peace. You have given me more than enough affection."

"Then what is the matter, my daughter?" Resi Bagaspati pressed.

Pujawati, the innocent child, finally came clean. She told her father all about her dreams. Her dreams were so vivid that she even knew the name of the knight. It was Narasoma of Mandaraka, who had filled her heart.

Resi Bagaspati was touched and very happy to hear of his daughter's dreams. Although she was only a mountain girl, living her life in the middle of the jungle, but in her heart has grown love, like a normal human being. Resi Bagaspati was sure that it was a match destined by the gods. He promised his daughter to find the knight to the ends of the earth and bring him to her.

Resi Bagaspati immediately began his journey. He shot himself into the air and looked down, trying to find the knight of his daughter's dreams. After so many days looking for the figure of a knight who was described by his daughter, Resi Bagaspati began to think it was a fruitless search. When he was about to go home in defeat, Resi Bagaspati met Narasoma in his journey. Overjoyed, the good Resi Bagaspati told him of his daughter's dreams and invited Narasoma to come to his hermitage. However, the prince of Mandaraka arrogantly refused.

"Bah! Who, in their right mind, would be willing to marry a giant! " He scoffed.

Surprised by this answer, Resi Bagaspati looked down on his own form. Yes, he remembered now. He was indeed a giant. It seemed funny that living with his daughter in blissful love all these years had made him forget how ugly he looked. This realisation brought a little tear to his eyes. His beautiful daughter loved him so completely that she never once asked him of his appearance. Even after seeing the handsome Narasoma in her dreams, her love for her giant father was unwavering.

Shaking off this reverie, Resi Bagaspati gently assured Narasoma that his daughter was very beautiful, because she was a descendant of a heavenly goddess. But all of Resi Bagaspati's words fell on deaf ears. Narasoma did not believe that anyone beautiful would ever deign to have a child with a giant. The good Resi did not give up. He tried and tried to persuade Narasoma to come with him and meet his daughter. After a while, Narasoma became angry. The prince of Mandaraka released his arrows towards the impudent giant. The whizzing arrows rained upon Resi Bagaspati's body. The wise man did not move from where he stood, merely brushed the arrows away from his body.

None of Narasoma's arrows were able to penetrate the skin of Resi Bagaspati. Narasoma got angrier. So, he swiftly got off his horse and charged into Resi Bagaspati. A battle between the prince and the kindly giant ensued. Narasoma was quite capable in terms of battle. He was a powerful knight of his country, well respected among foreign knights. However, Resi Bagaspati did not fight him seriously, because he did not want Narasoma, who had become the idol of his daughter's heart, to get hurt. Resi Bagaspati fought Narasoma long enough to test the skills of his future son-in-law. Soon, he ended the fight, with a magic spell, he paralyzes Narasoma. The prince of Mandaraka dropped to the ground, and Resi Bagaspati easily carried him to his hermitage.

Narasoma regained his consciousness in the home of Resi Bagaspati and his daughter. The first face he saw was the beautiful face of Pujawati. The voice of love in his heart could not be denied, and he fell instantly in love with her. The young couple were then married by Resi Bagaspati himself, and spent their honeymoon period at the hermitage.

Despite the joy in his heart that he was able to find a beautiful and devoted wife, Narasoma felt uneasy. Every time he was near his father –in-law, Narasoma felt ill at ease. Narasoma knew, although he refused to admit it, that he still could not accept the fact that he was now related to a giant, no mater how kindly. Whenever his father-in-law asked when Narasoma would take Pujawati to Mandaraka, Narasoma always evaded giving him any definite answer. His excuse was that he still wanted to enjoy the peaceful ways of the hermitage.

Every day, Narasoma would go hunting to avoid Resi Bagaspati. Sometimes he would left his wife for days, just so he would not see his father in law. Pujawati, although she kept silent about the matter, felt very lonely. She wanted to spend time with her new husband, enjoying beautiful days together on the distant hills full of flowers, on the mountains of Argabelah. Resi Bagaspati perceived this, and he was likewise very concerned with his son-in-law's attitude towards his beautiful wife.

One day, Pujawati was sitting in front of their little cottage, awaiting her husband who had not come home. Her father was also gone, trying to look for Narasoma, worried that his son-in-law maybe lost in the wood. Suddenly, Pujawati was surprised by the arrival of a hermit who showed her an arrow and asked if she recognized it. Anxiously, she admitted that she knew who the arrow belonged to. It was her husband's.

"Then, I want your husband to cut his finger to replace my fingers. If your husband does not want to account for his actions, I would curse him by the gods in order to punish him! " the hermit said furiously.

Unbeknownst to Narasoma himself, when he shot his arrows in his hunt, one of his arrow had struck the hermit and cut of his fingers. Before the hermit could recover himself and find him, Narasoma had continued his journey, unaware that he had injured anyone.

Pujawati, despite Narasoma's neglect, indeed loved her husband. She did not want him hurt in any way. Therefore, without hesitation, she cut off her own finger as an apology on behalf of her husband. She was devotion itself.

That night, Resi Bagaspati returned, unsuccessful in his task of finding Narasoma. Imagine his surprise when he saw that one of Pujawati's finger was missing. After hearing her story, Resi Bagaspati was furious. However, he was very much touched by Pujawati's loyalty towards her husband. He commended his daughter and gave her a new name, Setyawati, which means "loyalty."

In a cave in the wilderness, the hermit sat in front of the fire of worship, happy because his fingers had now been completed by Pujawati's finger. Suddenly, from the flame of the fire of worship materialized the giant face of Resi Bagaspati looking back at him with menacing eyes.

"Hermit! You may complain to Brahma, even to Yamadipati. They would not be able to take my life! Restore the finger of my daughter, or I will destroy your place of worship and kill you! "

This brought fear to the hermit. He knew of the name Resi Bagaspati, and he did not know that Pujawati was the daughter of this great giant. The hermit immediately cut Pujawati's finger from his hand. Such is the story of the loyalty of Pujawati to her husband, and Bagaspati's love to his daughter.

After Resi Bagaspati told Narasoma, who had returned home, of the incident, Narasoma vowed to never again leave his wife. Resi Bagaspati was happy, because Narasoma and Setyawati finally could live together as a real couple. To give them a chance to be together, Resi Bagaspati undertook to hunt, replacing Narasoma so Narasoma could be at home with his wife.

However, Narasoma was still ill at ease. One day, he gave his wife a riddle, enough to make her curious. He told Setyawati to ask her father for the answer.

One day, Setyawati asked her father, "Father, my husband gave me this enigma. I know it is nothing but a puzzle to tease me, but I am curious. He always refused to tell me what it means, and told me to ask you."

"What is it, daughter?" Resi Bagaspati asked her.

"A dish of warm, fragrant white rice is very delicious. But there is a grain that is tucked between the ripe rice. Pray, father, what does it mean?"

Bagaspati took a deep breath. He already knew the meaning. He did not suspect that all this time Narasoma considered him, Resi Bagaspati, as the grain that spoilt the beauty of his loving marriage to Setyawati. He now knew why all this time, Narasoma kept his distance and never wanted to take his wife home to meet his own parents. He was embarrassed to have a giant as a father-in-law. Bagaspati loved his daughter, and would give her anything to make her happy. Maybe his death would be the best way for his daughter's happiness, and the best way to end the curse of Batara Guru.

Bagaspati whispered to his beloved daughter to call Narasoma immediately, and asked her to prepare a set of tools and offerings ceremony.

"I would like to give my son-in-law my dragon magic which has been inside of me for many years now." He said with a sad smile.

Setyawati immediately obeyed her father's command.

When Setyawati was busy preparing the instruments for the ritual, Narasoma face Resi Bagaspati. His heart was restless, full of questions of what his father-in-law will say to him.

"Narasoma, I will try to give you an answer to riddle which you gave Setyawati. I will answer it in front of you, so that everything becomes clear, nothing else would be buried, and no one would be blamed. I will also give you the magic of the dragon. But before that, I ask you to promise me, to take care of Setyawati, love her with all your heart. You should not neglect her, even though she's just a mountain girl with no royal blood. She is a good girl, obediennt and very loyal to you. Do not forget this promise, for all your days."

Narasoma could not look at Resi Bagaspati. He was ashamed of himself, of his cowardly approach to his own father-in-law who had done nothing but love his daughter, and therefore welcoming himself to his family with open arms. With trembling lips, he tried to force himself take an oath before the Resi.

"Resi ... By heaven and earth, I vow not to neglect Setyawati. I love her with all my heart in life and death." That was all he was able to say.

That was enough for Resi Bagaspati. He then explain the magic spell that will be passed down to Narasoma. The name of the dragon's magic was *Candrabhirawa*. *Candra* means moon and *Bhirawa* implies darkness. It means 'the moon that illuminates the darkness'. It was like the light of the hearts of those who are wise, the light that comes out of the heart reflects the strength that is not owned by any other beings. The light which softens the rigors of a human hearts and minds, to form a civilization that is useful to the universe, then be someone who is able to reassure and protect others.

Resi Bagaspati reminded Narasoma that the magic of Candrabhirawa was very powerful, so it should not be used to exalt himself, or used with lust and greed.

Narasoma listened to his father-in-law in silence. Tears streaming down his face. The more he heard of the good Resi's gentle voice, the more he realized how pure the heart of this giant before him.

The evening grew increasingly late. The moon shone bright with the stars decorating the night. Little by little the clouds began to diminish the moonlight. As Setyawati returned with the equipment for the offering requested by her father, she saw the giant body of Resi Bagaspati, lifeless, in the arms of her husband who cried bitterly, as a son who had lost a father.

www.ingramcontent.com/pod-product-compliance
Lightning Source LLC
Chambersburg PA
CBHW070917180526
45168CB00005B/2047